The Socratic Parent

The
SOCRATIC
PARENT

How to Raise a Child of Any Age
by Asking the Right Questions

PAUL SWEETOW

The Socratic Parent: How to Raise a Child of Any Age by Asking the Right Questions

Book cover by difrats

Printed in the United States of America

www.TheSocraticParent.com

For everyone guiding a child through life

Acknowledgments

My parents, Herb and Bobbie, grew up in a generation that didn't use Socratic Parenting techniques, but they gave me all the tools to develop this method. They showered me with love and support. My memories of our dinner table involved my parents always engaging me about life and the local politics they were involved in. Without their having encouraged me to get involved, make a difference, and take healthy risks, this book would never have existed.

Sharon Heller's contributions to the flow and clinical aspects of this book were tremendous. As a developmental psychologist, author, and editor, she brought a wealth of knowledge and experience to this work.

Kira Freed has edited several books of mine, and I'm honored to work with her again. She is exceptional and simply the best at her craft. She edited the grammar and flow as well as creating the interior look and feel of this book. Kira also has a keen eye and feel for the delivery and reception of *The Socratic Parent*. I am deeply grateful for all she has done.

I was incredibly fortunate to have this book reviewed by a parent, and Elona Balyasny went above and beyond what I had hoped for. Her review of this book gave me deep insights into what parents would want included. Elona blended her parenting experience and keen intellect to help shape this book. I'm so thankful to her.

Jacob Sweetow, my son, was the recipient of my parenting successes and many blunders. I used the Socratic Parenting method with him over the years as I was developing it. He took to it and was my inspiration to continue creating what is now in your hands.

Contents

Preface

Parenting today is tougher than ever. Technology, social media, and video games have likely hijacked your kids. Schools can be dangerous, children are getting bullied online, and the world may feel like a scarier place. Many demands are placed on your time, and the list goes on.

You need adaptable skills to know how best to discipline, support, influence, and communicate with your children. Unfortunately, as every parent knows, the job does not come with a manual to guide you on how best to acquire these skills.

Socratic Parenting can help. The lessons in this book are incredibly easy and effective in helping you master these skills and strengthen your relationship with your children.

Essentially, Socratic Parenting involves asking your children thoughtful questions that help them form healthy life goals and connected action strategies, as well as boosting their self-esteem. That's it—and it's highly effective and easy to implement in your everyday life. I've taught this approach to the hundreds of parents with whom I've worked, and the feedback is overwhelmingly positive and life-changing.

The best part is that your children learn to take ownership of their goals and behaviors, which allows them to improve their relationships and choices now as well as glide much more easily into adulthood later.

Let's get started.

Introduction:
Benefits of Socratic Parenting

Pete and Susan's son, Joshua, was in third grade. Joshua was a loving and kind child who would often become frustrated. For example, when he lost at a video game, he would have a temper tantrum and scream at the game.

His parents told him not to worry, and when that was unsuccessful, they tried giving him time-outs. When Joshua's tantrums got extreme, with swearing and throwing the controller, they yelled at him to stop yelling. None of the methods they tried worked.

As Joshua's parents, they wanted to support and soothe their son. I suggested they try Socratic Parenting (SP).

Defining SP

The goal of SP is to teach your children to think for themselves. SP does so by focusing on sharing dialogues with your children, asking open-ended questions, and modeling the behaviors you want to see in your children. By using these approaches, your children will naturally want to become self-disciplined and independent thinkers. They will feel heard, valued, and supported.

Why Use Questions?

Asking open-ended questions has many benefits:

- Questions help parents gather information. For instance, you ask, "What did you enjoy about soccer today?"

- Questions help parents develop rapport with their kids. For example, you say, "I'm exhausted. I had a rough day at work. How was your day at school?" This question invites communication and discussion of feelings.

- Questions can encourage kids. For instance, you say, "I'm confident you can do it. What do you think?" You are planting in your children the belief that they can succeed.

- Questions help to uncover a child's state of mind. For example, you ask, "How did you feel after your test today?"

- Questions encourage flexible thinking by giving children different options and points of view. For instance, you ask, "What do you think about texting your friend and asking her to come over?" Though you are in essence offering advice, the question leaves the control in the child's hands.

- Questions serve as a mirror for children to understand themselves. For example, you ask, "Are you saying that you feel hurt by his remark?" This kind of question helps kids use feeling words to describe what is in their heart.

- Questions can help you understand your child's needs. For instance, "What would you like me to do to help you?" Or, "How can I best support you?"

- Questions help challenge children's limiting beliefs. For example, "Do you really think she threw the ball at you on purpose?" These kinds of questions help children think about whether someone wanted to harm them on purpose. They may come to the conclusion that it was just an accident.

Here are some sample questions to get you started:

- "What did you do today?"

- "What was your biggest challenge today? How did you feel about that challenge?"

- "What might you have said differently to your friend?"

- "What's another way of approaching your teacher?"

- "If you had a magic wand, what would you use it for?"

For an older child:

- "How did you improve someone else's life today?"

- "How did you take care of yourself today?"

Democratic Parenting

Instituting SP encourages parents to parent democratically. This parenting style offers the best outcome for children's growth.

Democratic parents parent with warmth and fairness. They treat their children as equals, meaning everyone in the family has a voice and is treated the same. Parents set the rules and consequences, and they explain and discuss them so children understand why they are in place.

Because they respect their children, democratic parents don't demand—instead, they request. They also ask questions of their children to find out what's happening. Consequently, children learn to become independent and to think for themselves.

First Step

Start by having your children state healthy goals in areas such as academics, relationships, wellness, and so on. Remember, for a child of any age, you can ask, "How can I best support you in achieving your goals?"

Young children: They can use "I like" or "I want" to state their goals.

School-age children: They can begin to state goals for the short-term future. "I'll practice my spelling words tonight for my quiz tomorrow."

Preteens and teens: They can state longer-term goals and begin to connect the future consequences, both good and bad, to their present-day behaviors.

Once your children have proclaimed positive goals, help them connect their actions to the goals that *they* want. Here are some suggestions:

Young children: "Wanting to do well in school is wonderful. How can you do that?"

Older children: "Great, you like feeling strong. How can you do that?" Or, "Getting good grades in school is a wonderful goal. What is your plan for doing it?"

Preteens and teens: "Great, you want to make more friends. How can you do that?"

If your children have specific action steps to achieve their goal, you are all set. If they don't, help them along with an either-or question such as, "What will get you more fit, riding your bicycle or playing video games?"

Using a reward system and charting their progress may be another useful tool to increase motivation and accountability.

Applying SP

Going back to Joshua, I said to the parents, "First, ask Joshua if he wants to be angry. He'll say no."

"Next, ask him how people can lose a game and not get too angry. Let's assume that he doesn't know. Before we share the answer with him, let's ask him questions to guide him to the right answer. It'll take more time, but it's worth the effort. If he comes up with the answer himself, he'll be more likely to use it."

"Because he's young," I said, "let's ask him with binary—either-or—types of questions. It will sound like this: 'Joshua, when you play with a friend, do you want the playdate to go well, or do you want to fight?'" The binary approach is useful for any age but especially children younger than twelve who have not yet fully developed their abstract thinking.

He'll say he wants it to go well. "Next, ask him, 'When you play games that have a winner and a loser, will you always win every game?'" He'll say no.

"'So, if you know that sometimes you'll lose, but at the same time you still want to have a great playdate, do you think it's a good idea to have a temper tantrum when you lose?' This question challenges limiting beliefs. Hopefully, he'll begin to see the connection and say no."

We used this same template to help Joshua with self-talk strategies to stay calm when he lost. I'd say, "When you lose, should you tell yourself, 'I can't stand it when I lose' or 'I don't like losing, but it's no big deal'?" This type of questioning helped him identify his self-talk and his feelings.

All this questioning helped Joshua have a great playdate by connecting his goals to his own actions: to be a good sport and to know that sometimes people win and sometimes they lose.

It wasn't always perfect, but Joshua became a better sport over time as he saw that his actions got him closer to attaining his goal of having great friendships. Because he formed goals and action steps that had good results, he used them more often and independently.

Avoid Advising

When using SP, in general it's best to give as little direct advice as possible. Ask yourself this question: What's best for your children when they are away from you and out in the world—the ability to solve problems for themselves or to rely on you to provide them with the answers?

When your children ask the right questions of themselves, the right answers will often be easily revealed. Remember that they will be making independent decisions much sooner than the age of eighteen. They'll make decisions about what they say and how they behave very early on at home, at school, and in your neighborhood.

Remember that direct advice and rules regarding safety issues are appropriate and necessary. Younger children will need directives such as "Don't put your finger in the electrical outlet," "Don't run across the street," and so on. As your children get older, you'll want to use more SP. You can tell your teenagers, "Don't drink alcohol." If they comply, great. You can also pose the question "What are the dangers of drinking or taking drugs?" This will lead them to consider the consequences when they are on their own.

PART I:
Parenting Style

Chapter 1

Keeping Strict Order

William, a forty-year-old construction worker, yelled at everyone in his family. When one of his children broke a rule, or if he and his wife disagreed, he would shout until he won the fight. To him, he was right and everyone else was wrong.

He also hit his kids, but mostly he was verbally abusive. Yet such psychological abuse, as it's called, can be just as damaging as striking a child.

The Authoritarian Parent

William was an authoritarian parent who went by the rule "It's my way or the highway."

Authoritarian parents keep order by setting strict rules that lack choices. They tend to bark orders without explanation and keep their kids on a short, unwavering leash. If a child asks for an explanation, the answer is typically "Because I said so."

Instead of using the Socratic method, authoritarian parents use directives. Here are examples that show the contrast between the two parenting methods.

Directive: Do your homework!
Socratic: What are the benefits of doing your homework?

Directive: Stop being disrespectful!
Socratic: Is that the kind of relationship you want with me?

Directive: Go to sleep on time!
Socratic: What are the benefits of getting a great night's sleep?

Directive: Treat your friends kindly.
Socratic: How do you want to treat your friends?

Directive: Stop having a temper tantrum.
Socratic: What is the benefit to you when you don't have a tantrum?

Directive: Do your chores.
Socratic: Should we all do our part to help our family?

When parents discipline without flexibility, and when control is imposed from without, children do not learn self-control or how to modify their behavior. As a result, children tend to be compliant, fearful, and submissive, and they possess low self-esteem.

Rather than being intrinsically motivated, they comply with parental demands out of fear of punishment or rejection and grow up seemingly independent, but inside they remain children desperately in need of love.

Typically they move out of the house as soon as possible. And then the parents wonder why their son or daughter never calls them.

Spanking

The American Pediatric Association has officially condemned spanking children. And, in my thirty years of work, I've never seen any abuse—verbal or physical—do anything but damage a child. If you are hitting or otherwise abusing your children, please stop and get professional help.

Along with yelling at their children, authoritarian parents may hit or spank them. Spanking is an undesirable way to get children to behave, for several reasons.

- It teaches children that might is right and that violence is an acceptable way to get what you want.

- It makes children feel powerless. To compensate, children might grow up and abuse others to feel a sense of power.

- Children who endure ongoing beatings as a consequence for a behavior begin to think "I'm bad" instead of thinking they made a bad choice in behaving a certain way. It is never good for children to believe they are bad. Remember, behavior can be bad, but children are not.

- Spanking is also painful for parents, who might feel like bullies. Such feelings lead to remorse, guilt, and doubts about the quality of their parenting skills.

- Spanking is disrespectful to children, and it doesn't teach respectful values or standards. Would you smack a coworker because he or she didn't do a good job, spoke out of turn, or disappointed you?

- Spanking breaks trust and children's sense of security that their parents love them and can be counted on to protect them from harm.

- Spanking is emotionally and physically abusive.

Below are other ways to discipline your children that work far better.

How to Manage Your Children's Behavior

Although SP aims to stoke intrinsic motivation and independence, the truth is that no one strategy always works. You will also want to use extrinsic motivators from time to time—that is, rewards and consequences.

To begin, always inform children in advance of the family rules and the consequences of misbehavior. Make the consequence commensurate with the transgression. If taking a child's phone away for one night will help him or her stop a behavior, for example, you don't need to take it away for one month.

For young children, time-outs should be about one minute for each year of their age, so a five-year-old gets a five-minute time-out.

A consequence can be passive or active. A time-out and taking something away are passive, whereas cleaning the garage and vacuuming the rug are active.

Before you give consequences for bad behavior, it's always best to try to reward children for good behavior. It's preferable to have the reward be an experience, such as breakfast with Mom. It's okay to use money or items as rewards, but try to offer experiences as much as possible.

Have a plan. Don't come up with consequences in the heat of the moment. Rewards and consequences are meant to increase or decrease a behavior—not for you to get even. Don't use them for that reason.

Don't deliver a consequence angrily. Start with a warning that a certain behavior will lead to a previously planned consequence. You can say, "That's warning number 1," "That's warning number 2," and "You've had two warnings. Now you have chosen to get the consequence."

Be predictable and consistent.

William Meets His Match

Sometimes a child has the same combative temperament as a parent, which can lead to a parent and child locking horns. Such was the case with William and his seven-year-old son, Ryan, who would also yell and not back down.

William would scream at Ryan, "Turn off the video game."

"No. Leave me alone," Ryan would yell back.

Not believing this small child had the nerve to fight back and even be willing to raise the volume, William screamed louder than Ryan, "You little sh-t, you do what I tell you and don't talk back."

Ryan responded, "No, and you are a bigger sh-t."

William told me, "Every time Ryan gets upset, he starts screaming, and I can't stand it. The only way to get him to see who's boss is for me to scream louder, so that's what I do, and that's not even working anymore. Plus, now Ryan is screaming at his sister and even his friends. He's running out of friends because they don't want to be with him anymore."

William went on to say, "I love my family, but everything feels like it's falling apart. Being at work is calmer than coming home, and now I dread walking in the door after a long day at work."

I explained to William that yelling at Ryan was him (William) having his own temper tantrum. He can't get his way, so he gets angry and screams, as he equates disobedience with lack of respect. Further, when his own child doesn't behave, William feels like a weak person.

Radical Acceptance

I told William that the solution to reducing his own rage was to practice radical acceptance. Radical acceptance is about accepting life as it comes and not resisting what you cannot or choose not to change. In William's case, he couldn't change his son's character.

The notion of acceptance is significantly different from approving a behavior. With acceptance, you simply observe the reality as it actually is, without judgment. Approval, on the other hand, means to sanction or authorize. When we make judgment calls about whether or not to approve things, we assert our position as people in authority.

Parents don't have to, and shouldn't, approve of bad behavior—just accept that it happened. William could disapprove of Ryan's behavior as something he didn't want, but he had to accept that it actually happened. Acceptance would prevent William from reacting too quickly and would give him pause to choose a better response.

The bottom line: People need food, water, air, and shelter. All the rest are wants. William needed to learn the difference between needs and wants.

And, in fact, Ryan was simply modeling the behaviors he learned from his dad. When he was involved in a disagreement, he knew how to take an adversarial stance and fight. He also knew there would be a winner and a loser.

Things started to turn around when William began employing SP with Ryan. Here's an example of a conversation:

William: Ryan, I know video games are fun and they are hard to stop playing. Would it help you if I gave you a reminder ten minutes before you have to turn off the game?

Ryan: Yeah, then I can finish my game.

William: Okay, great. Do you think you might still get upset when it's time to turn off the game?

Ryan: Yeah, because I love playing video games.

William: I understand that they are fun and that it's hard to turn them off. What's the best way for us not to fight when you have to turn off the game?

Ryan: I don't know.

William: Well, I want us to be kind and loving to each other. So, I'll stay calm and not yell. But if I need to, I'll turn off the game from my computer's control system that can shut your game off.

Ryan: Okay, but I'll try to turn it off on time.

With this conversation, William related to Ryan's difficulty in turning off the game and also set firm limits without yelling. William had a plan in case Ryan was noncompliant, which was to use a parental control hub. This is software that connects to your home router to restrict any device's access to the Internet with time-based rules. It's a tool every parent should have installed. With a plan in place for both father and son, their relationship improved dramatically.

William liked the SP method when it was coupled with a plan to set limits if needed.

The Lesson: Every parent experiences frustration, and everyone loses their temper from time to time. Increasing demands on your child will not solve the problem—they will only intensify your frustration. Other solutions, such as SP, work better.

The Takeaway: Using SP and radical acceptance will help reduce anger and benefit both parent and child. That's known as a win/win.

Chapter 2

The Permissive Parent

Steve and Marie were loving, well-educated parents who were having some trouble with their five-year-old daughter, Emma. She was noncompliant to their directions and would not follow their advice. Even simple tasks like brushing her teeth before bedtime led to fights.

Marie said, "I tell her she has to listen and obey me because I am her mother, but she doesn't. I then tell her I will count to five, and if she doesn't brush her teeth, she won't be allowed to play her video game. But she's stubborn and still doesn't budge. So I give her another chance and count to five again."

Steve jumped in, "Yeah, and when that happens, I need to get involved, and I scream at her. She either screams back or starts to cry. Then I feel bad and hug her because I don't like to see her cry. This happens during a variety of tasks that we tell her to do almost every day."

Marie said, "Our home is loud and angry, and I'm incredibly stressed. I thought being a mom was going to be fun, but honestly, I'm not enjoying it at all."

Steve added, "Now it's affecting our marriage. We don't always agree on what to do with Emma, and we're fighting and yelling at each other."

Steve and Marie meant well, but they were clueless about how to parent Emma.

Permissive Parents

When children rule the roost, there's a good chance that the parents are permissive.

Permissive parents are lenient and adopt a laissez-faire or hands-off approach, relating to their children more like friends than authority figures.

It may seem as though children would love such freedom, but they don't. Children cannot take care of themselves and need the security of knowing the rules and boundaries of their behavior. If no one is giving them guidance and setting down rules, they feel insecure and unprotected.

Consequently, they have mixed feelings about their parents and develop ambivalent attachments. They love their parents for their warmth and affection but, unable to rely on their parents to meet their needs, they feel angry and mistrustful of them.

Nor do these kids turn out well. Ultimately, too much autonomy and independence create immature, insecure, irresponsible, out-of-control children who don't follow rules or know how to behave in social situations. In place of the parents, siblings, friends, teachers, and eventually police officers and judges are forced to set limits, enforce consequences, and offer guidance.

Steve and Marie both grew up "old school" with authoritarian parents. Their parents set down rules, and if the rules were broken, they got spanked. This made them afraid of their parents, and they learned early on to be obedient or face the violent consequences. To this day, their relationships with their parents are strained. They get together with them for the holidays but never make an effort to see them at other times of the year.

Both Steve's and Marie's parents encouraged them to spank Emma until she submitted to them. Thankfully, Steve and Marie didn't follow their parents' advice. However, because their parents had been so strict, they decided to do the opposite with their child and easily gave in to her.

Parents Were Clueless

Since Steve and Marie experienced little autonomy during their childhoods—the freedom to make independent decisions—they didn't know how to guide Emma to make good choices and follow some basic rules.

I suggested some strategies to help Emma become more autonomous. They both looked at me as though I was crazy. "She's only five years old! She's not autonomous, she's not setting the rules, and we're not going to let her rule our house."

"Great," I said, "then we are all on the same page. Let me suggest a few ways to get to a win/win. Use Socratic Parenting. The sooner Emma begins to make healthy choices on her own, the better. Besides, she's already somewhat autonomous when she's on the playground dealing with other kids and chooses her own words and actions, much as she does at home.

"Try saying this to her: 'Emma, do you want to have clean, strong teeth or dirty, rotten teeth?'"

"By giving Emma a choice," I continued, "you'll help her become more intrinsically motivated. Choices give children a say in what they want and in how to accomplish goals."

Intrinsic vs. Extrinsic Motivation

Intrinsic motivation is the desire to do something for an internal reward—in other words, engaging in a behavior because it is naturally satisfying to you. Extrinsic motivation, in contrast, involves doing something to get a reward or avoid a consequence.

Ideally, we want to encourage intrinsic motivation in children. When children are intrinsically motivated, they use:

- Independent thinking

- Self-direction, meaning they are able to do things by themselves

- The power of positive thinking, because intrinsic motivation gives children an "I can" attitude and builds self-confidence

If Emma says the correct answer—"clean, strong teeth"—great. Your next Socratic question would be: "Do you know how to keep your teeth clean and strong?"

Now, if she says that she doesn't care or prefers dirty, rotten teeth as long as she gets to skip brushing them at night, then ask, "Hmm . . . well, what's the good part of having dirty, rotten teeth?" I call this a *paradoxical question*, and it can be quite powerful.

Paradoxical Questioning

Paradoxical questioning dives deeper into the rewards and consequences of your child's bad choice. It also provides a bit of shock value and may awaken some deeper thinking. "What's the benefit of not studying?" "Why is it a good idea not to study tonight?" "Why is it a good idea to hit your friend when you lose a game?" The purpose here is to highlight that while there may be some immediate gratification, in the long run those choices will be much worse.

Let her consider that, and resist giving her the correct answer. At this age, Emma doesn't fully understand the long-term consequences of not brushing her teeth. That level of abstract thinking isn't yet developed enough.

You can help her by showing her a picture of clean teeth and a picture of rotten teeth to help her visualize. But don't scream, "DO YOU SEE WHAT WILL HAPPEN IF YOU DON'T BRUSH YOUR TEETH?!" Instead ask, "Which picture do you want your teeth to look like?"

Just let her think about it, even for a few days if need be, and try to be positive. Say, "Emma, you are so smart, and I will love you no matter what color your teeth are."

As it turned out, Emma was stubborn for a full week, and Steve and Marie were beginning to doubt my advice. I encouraged them to stick with it a while longer. The following week, Emma stated that she was going to brush her teeth because she liked the way her minty breath smelled. Later we learned that some kids were telling her that her breath was stinky!

Both the Socratic Parenting and the natural consequence from other kids helped Emma change her behavior. She began brushing her teeth because she wanted to, and she noticed the benefits.

Harry

Matthew and Jessica, parents of six-year-old Harry, were another example of permissive parenting.

Harry was wearing them down with constant negotiating to get his way. And, as with Emma, he often won.

"What is his negotiating like?" I asked his mom.

"Well, it goes something like this," Jessica said.

Harry: Mom, can I play video games now?

Mom: No, we agreed not on school nights.

Harry: Please. Mom—I was so good today.

Mom: No, and please don't ask me again. I'm tired.

Harry: But Mom, I got all of my homework done. Pleeease.

Mom: Ugh, I said no.

After the tenth time that Harry pleaded, Jessica would say, "All right, just this once."

As you can see, Jessica was another permissive, wishy-washy parent. The problem was that she was using intermittent reinforcement, which I proceeded to share about with her.

"What's that?" Jessica asked.

"Well," I said, "you are essentially rewarding him for never giving up. This lets him know that eventually he will get a reward as long as he keeps asking. So, the intermittent reinforcement should stop."

Both mother and father understood. They stopped their intermittent reinforcement and began to be consistent. When they did, Harry amped up his asking and negotiating for three full days.

I told his parents to expect this and to make sure to present a united front and be supportive of each other. "Stay consistent and firm, but don't get angry. Harry is only acting rationally."

They also instituted SP. Here's an example:

Matthew: Harry, do you understand why we don't let you play video games on school nights?

Harry: No.

Matthew: Because we want you to enjoy other activities besides video games. And, we think playing video games on the weekends is enough time for that.

Harry: Nope. I want to play every day. It's fun.

Jessica: We understand that you feel that way. We want you to enjoy video games and also do other things like sports, music, and being with us. Do you think you would enjoy those other activities?

Harry: Yeah. But not as much as video games.

Jessica: If you only play video games, do you think giving up all the other things in your life is good for you?

Harry: Well, no—I want to play soccer, and I like to draw, too.

Matthew: That's great—we know you're talented in many ways! It's going to be exciting to try other activities.

Eventually, after seven days, Harry reduced his fighting. He was grittier than we anticipated, but as long as Matthew and Jessica made sure not to give in, Harry began to predict the outcome and stopped fighting.

The Lesson: When children learn that they can wear you down and eventually get their way, they won't stop. Harry thinks, "If I ask my mom a hundred times, she eventually says yes, so I need to keep going until she says yes."

To fix intermittent reinforcement, keep your rules simple, consistent, and predictable. Don't change them on the fly or when you're worn out. If you can't follow through with enforcing a rule, revise it.

Also, when you first stop the intermittent reinforcement, expect your children to whine and negotiate more intensely to try and win. Stay calm, consistent, and predictable. With time, your children will stop negotiating and fighting.

The Takeaway: Be consistent and predictable, and follow through. Don't use intermittent reinforcement.

Chapter 3

Practice
What You Preach

In this chapter, I'm not going to present an SP session. Rather, I will talk about the need for parents to be models for their children, which is an essential component of SP.

Your children will observe how you handle everything—from daily habits to daily annoyances, unfair occurrences, life setbacks, obstacles, and working through issues with others—and model what you do. When they see you reading, they're more inclined to become readers. Likewise, when they see you drinking alcohol, they're more inclined to drink alcohol.

Lawrence and Miles

Lawrence and his son, Miles, are a great example of modeling. A loving father and former college football star, Lawrence was forty-five years old and still in great physical shape from his consistent workouts.

His son, Miles, loved to exercise, too. It was a way for him to spend time with his dad, and he loved the improvement that his consistent workouts were bringing.

Lawrence and Miles talked about exercise at times, but mostly they did it, unlike other dads of Miles's friends, who talked about sports but didn't engage in them. Miles felt lucky to spend this time with his dad as they exercised together.

Miles shared with me how much he wished to model himself after his dad—and his mom as well, a doctor who also exercised and who read a lot. He was surrounded by parents who were healthy and smart, and he naturally did what they demonstrated.

My Son and I

When Jacob was in first grade, I said, "Hey, let's do 10 push-ups every day for a year. It'll just take us about 30 seconds a day. At the end of the year, we will have done 3,650 push-ups."

Jacob, who liked to do what I did, said, "Sure." I then made a simple spreadsheet and put it on the refrigerator. It had a box to check off each day we completed 10 push-ups.

Some days, we were tired and didn't feel motivated to do push-ups. It didn't matter how we felt. As long as I was willing to do the push-ups, Jacob would imitate me, and it became our morning routine before breakfast.

The Lesson: *Practice what you preach.* We've heard this cliché a million times. Yet it's so true. From an early age, your children will observe you and mimic your habits, your emotions, your responses, and so on.

For this reason, "Do as I say, not as I do" doesn't work. Your children will notice the conflicting advice and won't respect you when you tell them this.

The Takeaway: Live and model the life you want your children to live.

Take a Break from Your Children

You've heard the saying "Put on your oxygen mask first on an airplane." To function well as a parent and be someone your children will respect and want to model, you need to take care of yourself. If not, you may feel resentful at times and be more likely to become angry and lose your temper.

One way to take care of your own needs is to take breaks from your children to recharge.

Nick and Katrina were attentive and loving parents, and their kids were doing well. They would spend every moment parenting their four children. For eight years, the couple never went on a vacation without their children and never had a date night without their children. Their youngest slept in their bed at night.

The parents were starting to get burned out, and they felt guilty about it. They said, "We had children because we wanted them in our lives. Now we look forward to their bedtime."

Soon this burnout began to reduce their patience with their children as well as with their marriage. They were fighting more than ever and feeling discouraged.

Further, Nick and Katrina were inadvertently setting a poor example of a healthy marriage. Children can tolerate time away from their parents and may even learn some useful lessons for their future romantic lives.

I gave Nick and Katrina the homework to have two date nights per month. They were able to ask a grandparent to watch the children from 6 to 10 p.m.— enough time for a nice night out. Within a few months, Nick and Katrina felt reconnected in their marriage and recharged with their children.

For a portion of their date night, I encouraged Nick and Katrina to use this five-step template for a connected discussion:

1. Share news and current going-ons with each other. This doesn't need to be deeply emotional—it can simply be what is going on in each of your lives.

2. What are you curious to know about each other?

3. What are you grateful for about each other?

4. Share a complaint or problem, along with a solution. Don't complain without offering a solution. Commit this phrase to memory: *Don't win the fight—solve the problem.*

5. What are your hopes and wishes for yourself, each other, and the relationship?

The Lesson: All relationships require your energy. When you are in a constant state of expending energy, you will burn out. You need recovery to recharge. So be sure and take time for both yourself and your spouse.

The Takeaway: Take a break and recharge your energy.

PART II:

Parenting Your Child to Succeed

Chapter 4

Promote Independence in Your Child

Allow Your Child to Be Independent

Mary is a loving mother who is deeply connected to her son, Joey. She began our meeting saying, "'We're having a hard time with anxiety and making friends. Every night 'we' worry at bedtime, and 'we' can't fall asleep."

I asked Joey how he felt. He looked at his mother for approval before speaking. Then without breaking eye contact with his mother, he said, "Yeah, I am feeling worried at night." He nodded to his mother as if to ask, "Did I say the right thing?"

I asked Mary, "Are you having anxiety at night, too? You mentioned that you were both anxious."

"Oh yes," Mary said, "When Joey is anxious, I'm anxious. When he's happy, I'm happy. And, when he's sad, I'm sad, too."

"Is that why you speak of Joey as 'we' rather than 'he'?"

Mary winced as if taken aback by my blunt question.

I said, "Clearly, you feel connected in a loving way to Joey, but let's honor both of you as two individuals. When Joey's feeling and efforts are his own, he is empowered." I taught Mary about SP, and she agreed to try it. She reported back that her conversation went well.

Here's what she said:

Mary: Joey, I think you're smart and talented, and I love you so much. Would you like to feel less worried?

Joey: I love you too, Mom, and yes, I want to feel less worried.

Mary: Great. I'll help you, but you'll do a lot of the work on your own. This way, you can use the plan to feel less worried anytime we are not together, like at school.

Joey: That sounds great!

The Lesson: It's not unusual for a parent to refer to his or her child in the plural by using "we." Much of a child's early life is dependent on his or her parent(s). Children couldn't survive or get anything done without a "we" relationship. But they soon grow into toddlers and have to begin their own lives as independent people—with you alongside them. Saying "We have homework to do," "We need to be nicer to our friends," and so on robs children of their autonomy and rings false.

Children need to hear "he" or "she" when you speak about them. The use of a pronoun honors their individual life and empowers them to grow, feel safe, learn, and explore. Yes, your parental guidance and support are still critical for their development, but let your children do their work, succeed, and struggle on their own and build their resilience and confidence.

The only time I have found it appropriate and even useful to use "we" is when a child is going through serious medical treatment or some other trauma. In those cases, parents feel deeply connected to the experience, and using "we" helps children feel less alone.

The Takeaway: Drop the "we" and honor the "he" or "she."

Don't Spoil Your Child

Beth was the mother of fourth-grade twins John and Trisha. Having grown up in an affluent home, she inherited a lot of money. John and Trisha were given an abundance of material items and were spoiled. Whatever they wanted, Beth would buy it for them. She'd say, "Well, I can afford it, and if it makes them happy, why not?"

John and Trisha would easily tire of what they had, and Beth would always buy them more, hoping it would bring them lasting joy. But it didn't.

I suggested that Beth cut their allowance, urge her children to earn money by doing chores, and encourage them to pursue endeavors that required time and effort to master. Not only was this experience lacking in her children's lives, but it was also absent from Beth's life. Beth was willing to try some SP as well. The conversation with her children went like this:

Beth: John and Trisha, I love you two so much and want you to be happy. Have you heard the phrase "money can't buy happiness"?

John: Yeah.

Trisha: We've heard that before.

Beth: What do you think it means?

Trisha: Well, I think it means that material stuff can't make people feel happy.

John: Yeah.

Beth: As you know, I grew up with a lot of money, and my parents spoiled me. For a short while,

I enjoyed the items, but I never really felt happy because of them. I spent so much of my life thinking that buying items would bring happiness. It never did. How do you two feel about it?

Trisha: Well, we definitely enjoy shopping and would like to continue.

John: Yeah, I don't really want to stop shopping either.

Beth: I get it. But do you think it would be good for you to experiment for one month with not buying anything just to see how you feel?

Trisha: Yeah, we would try that.

John: Yep. That's okay.

The Lesson: Money can't buy happiness and may cause our children to lose sight of what is important. Instead, teach your children the values they will need to become successful in life by encouraging hard work, diligence, and responsibility.

When you do want to buy them something, consider buying items that will foster deeper talents requiring effort. For example, consider items like musical instruments, lessons, sport equipment, and the like. An abundance of clothing, fancy toys, and the newest devices won't really bring much value to your children.

The Takeaway: Even if you can afford it, say no to an abundance of purchases. Replace them with experiences that you can share together and make memories.

Chapter 5

Praise Efforts over Results

Ken and Maya were loving parents, and they were both Type A personalities. High achievers in both their professional and personal lives, they naturally also parented that way. They were results-driven and measured their lives based on that approach.

Their son, Jason, was in seventh grade and was doing well enough in school, with a mix of A's and B's. He was a good soccer player, though not the best on his team. On most days, he was generally happy.

Ken and Maya felt that Jason was not living up to his potential, and this frustrated them. They felt he could be a straight-A student and an all-star soccer player if he put in more effort. They constantly expressed their disappointment in him for not meeting their very high standards. Ken and Maya never considered that their standards might not be realistic or achievable. Further, their standards may not be in line with Jason's own goals and passions.

Jason wasn't opposed to getting better results, but his parents' demands were stressing him out because he worried that he was disappointing them. The more he worried, the more he disliked working harder. He might also have been holding back from success. Jason knew what it felt like to have his parents disappointed in him when he wasn't trying as hard as he could. He worried about what his parents would think if he tried his best and still failed.

I suggested that Jason could just focus on his efforts and not the results. At first, Ken and Maya were unhappy with my suggestion, reiterating that life is all about results, not effort. I agreed that positive results were desirable and that it was important for Jason to learn that better results often occur with more effort.

They agreed to try focusing on effort instead of results for three months to see how that worked. I encouraged them to use SP with Jason. Their conversation went like this:

Ken: Jason, we are really proud of you and love you so much. Would it be okay if we stopped pressuring you to be perfect?

Jason: Yeah, I'd really like that. When you pressure me so much, I get upset.

Maya: Okay, then. We still believe you should try your best. How about we agree that your effort is most important, not your results?

Jason: Does that mean I need to always try my best?

Maya: Well, what would be the advantage for you if you try your best?

Jason: I'd probably do pretty good at school because I'm smart.

Ken: Yes! You are really smart. How about we all just focus on trying our best and let the results be whatever they are?

Jason: That sounds really good.

Ken and Maya later said things like: "Nice hustle at practice" and "We noticed you studied an extra hour for your math test—way to go!" Regardless of the outcomes, the efforts were praised.

As you can guess, Jason's results improved.

The Lesson: Praising effort over results has benefits.

- Effort is daily, even moment-to-moment. Results such as grades and wins/losses at games occur less often.

- Praising effort in an honest way makes everyone feel good and makes children more likely to increase daily effort to get those compliments.

- Solid effort requires developing executive functioning skills, which are necessary for success in any endeavor.

- Parental guidance can focus on optimizing effort, for example, encouraging children to speak with their teacher about preparing for tests.

- Effort can continue after the results are in to review what went well and what needs improvement.

The Takeaway: Since genuine effort usually yields better results, praising effort over results is a good strategy to use when you want to have less stress and want your children to try harder. You can make a plan so the effort can be measured by your children.

Don't Overload Your Children with Improvements

When I first met Kyle and Julie, they began the conversation by focusing on a long list of improvements they wanted their daughter Shannon to make. Everything on their list was actually a good thing: going to bed on time, brushing her teeth, getting her homework done, cleaning the basement, drinking her milk, being nice to her sister, combing her hair, walking the dog, turning off the computer, sharpening her pencil, eating her veggies, and so on.

I told them that while these items were important, they presented endless demands for Shannon and would strain the relationship with unlimited conditions that she must meet. She might also have increased anxiety because their demands didn't have structure or predictability. Instead, I told them to first focus on the top two and then move down the list once those items are crossed off.

Kyle and Julie used SP to discuss this with Shannon:

Julie: Shannon, we love you so much, and we noticed that we are constantly asking you to do a lot of things. Have you noticed that, too?

Shannon: Wow, for sure—you guys are always telling me to do something. And as soon as I'm done with one thing, you want me to do something else.

Kyle: Would you like it if we just focused each day on you doing two things instead of ten?

Shannon: Yes!

Kyle: Okay, how about if we make a list of healthy things for you to do, but we will just ask you to do two of them?

Julie: Only after you know how to do a task by yourself will we move on to a new one.

Shannon: I love that idea. Then I can get really good at a couple of things at a time.

The top items on any list that a parent should focus on are health and safety. Julie and Kyle's list for Shannon looked like this:

- Safety

- Wellness

- Being kind

- Getting homework done by 8:30 p.m.

- Getting chores done

- Turning off devices by 9 p.m.

- Practicing piano for twenty minutes every day

- Making her own breakfast

Once Julie and Kyle agreed and just focused on the top two items, they were amazed at how less stressed everyone was. Many of the life skills they highlighted and worked on utilized *Student Life Skills*, a book I wrote filled with one-minute life-skill lessons. Shannon just had to focus on two items at a time and had plenty of time to enjoy her loving relationship with her parents.

The Lesson: We all have a long list of improvements to make. After all, life is busy, and there are always plenty of areas to improve on. Whether on paper or in your head, the list may feel overwhelming.

No worries—keep your list and just focus your time and energy on the first two items. Prioritize safety, urgency, and importance. Then, when those two are accomplished, cross them off and move down to the next two. And don't forget to celebrate accomplishments; even a simple "Nice job!" can have a very positive effect.

You only have so much time and energy to devote to parenting. The list can grow so long that it would be impossible to accomplish everything every day. So, pick the top two items to pour your energy into, and know that you can get to the other items later.

Again, with Socratic Parenting, many of the items on the list will be self-directed by your children, who will work on them independently. It's nice when children take care of themselves and the items on the list disappear without too much effort or guidance on your part. This is a very significant benefit of SP:

your children, step-by-step, become more indepen-dent and confident.

The Takeaway: Only focus on a few of the most important items on your list. Once those items are accomplished, move down the list, one item at a time.

Chapter 6

Promote Persistence

Patrick and Anne had two children: Steven, age eight, and Jessie, age six. Steven was feeling anxious and began avoiding things he had enjoyed in the past. For instance, he stopped going to basketball practice.

Steven knew his parents enjoyed coming to his games and cheering him on. But basketball was a challenge for him, and he was one of the weaker players. Working hard wasn't fun, because he didn't see the results he had hoped for from each practice.

Patrick and Anne saw the pain in their son and began to consider encouraging him to quit. I suggested that they let him struggle a bit and even endure some failure. By doing so, I predicted that some positive experiences would likely unfold. They agreed to have Steven finish the season.

Unfortunately, most of us underestimate the value of failure. We push our children for successful results, understandably, and forget that most of those successes will be born from failures.

There are two types of failure: failing backward and failing forward.

Failing backward involves having a negative result and then judging ourselves harshly. "I am no good." "I screwed up." "I hate myself." We see our children do this and want to eliminate their pain by letting them quit.

Failing forward, in contrast, is having a negative result and then observing without harsh judgment. "I made a mistake and will learn from it. I didn't prepare enough this time and will make more of an effort in the future." It's honest. You take responsibility without making excuses and without degrading yourself.

Failing forward is what parents need to encourage in children. When you let your children fail, you give them a gift. Lessons are learned, and resilience is built. Further, embracing effort over results fosters greater effort, which usually leads to better results and increased confidence and self-esteem.

If your children feel the pain of a failure, let them know you understand that failure is painful but not the end of the world. Also, let them know they can handle it and that things will be okay. These messages are illustrated in the following SP conversation between Steven and his parents:

Anne: Steven, we love that you play basketball. How are you enjoying it?

Steven: I don't like it. I'm not good at it.

Anne: Why do you feel that way?

Steven: It's so obvious. I can't dribble, and I've only made one basket in five games.

Anne: That must feel frustrating.

Steven: Yeah, and I want to quit. Can I?

Patrick: Well, we'd like you to finish the season that you committed to. We also don't want you to be afraid of making mistakes or even failing sometimes. Does that make sense?

Steven: No! Why do you want me to fail?

Patrick: Well, we don't *want* you to fail, but we don't want you to be afraid of failing, because you'll realize it's not the end of the world. What are the good and bad parts of quitting basketball?

Steven: If I quit, I no longer have to worry about playing badly, so that's good. But if I quit, I also won't have a chance to get better or make new friends.

Anne: And when you fail, how long are you upset for?

Steven: I'm mad for about a day.

Anne: Then your anger goes away?

Steven: Yeah, and sometimes it goes away after a few minutes.

Patrick: So, if you keep trying, you may get better, and even if you don't get better, your upset feelings go away pretty soon, right?

Steven: Yeah.

Patrick: Great. So we'd like you to stick with basketball for now and set a couple of realistic goals, like practicing dribbling for five minutes a day. How does that sound?

Steven: I guess that's okay. Even though I'm not so good now, I might get better, and I'm making friends. I like that.

Notice how Anne and Patrick also encouraged Steven to state the cost and benefits of his choice, including any negative consequences of not continuing to play basketball.

At the end of the season, Steven had not improved significantly, and he quit the sport. All was not lost, though. He felt good that, with his parents' support, he was able to handle the disappointment: it was bad but not horrible.

Steven also admitted that he didn't practice very hard or put in extra effort, and that was likely a reason he didn't improve much. But he had made some friends.

Also, he later tried a new sport: swimming. This sport suited him better, as it required less coordination and skill than basketball, which had physical requirements that didn't come naturally to him. Skill sports have a slower progression and require hours of technique repetition before competence is achieved. Some children excel more at sports that have less emphasis on precise technique, like swimming, running, and bicycling.

The Lesson: Give your children the opportunity to fail forward, learn lessons, and build grit and resilience.

Tolerating Discomfort

Don't immediately help children with problem-solving. Let them sit with the pain for a while and they'll learn not to be afraid of it. Life will have its down moments; we want our children to accept those moments, feel them, experience them, and learn that they pass with time. If children don't learn to experience those moments, they may use unhealthy means to avoid feeling pain—drinking, drugs, overeating, staring at a screen, or whatever they can use to get through the day.

The Takeaway: Let your children fail forward and live full lives with adventures and healthy risks.

Chapter 7

Promote Academic Excellence

Cole, a second grader, complained about his schoolwork. His parents tried Socratic Parenting and told him, "You're really smart, and we know you can learn anything. Would you like it if we didn't get upset and bother you about your homework?"

Cole said, "Yeah!"

"Great," they said. "We'll make you a deal: we won't bother you about schoolwork, and you get to decide whether or not you want to do it—no consequences from us."

He looked surprised and said, "Oh. Yeah."

They said, "Just one thing—if you choose not to do it, you must go to school and tell your teacher that you chose not to do it."

"And," they continued, "if you choose not to do it, you need to tell us the best part of not doing it and the worst part. That's all—we'll listen, and you get to decide."

Cole's parents rarely had to get on his case about schoolwork because Cole enjoyed the autonomy and the praise he received from his early successes. He got traction being independent, and he liked it. On occasion, his parents would gently remind him of his own goals, and they had to limit his video gaming because it was hard for Cole to turn it off. As the years went by, Cole did well in school, and it was not a major stressor for him or his parents.

The Lesson: Early on, teach the connection between academic success and future benefits—not just money, but also becoming smart and having more freedom to make choices later in life. Give children autonomy to get their work organized and completed independently. Allow them to advocate for themselves and communicate with teachers and coaches on their own. Resist the temptation to do it for them, and allow natural consequences to occur—both good and bad.

As always, you have a floor that you will not allow your children to sink below. If they actually completely shut down their academic effort, you would use rewards and negative consequences to shape their behavior.

The Takeaway: Socratic Parenting works well to help academic performance.

Chapter 8

Team Up with Your Child's Teacher

Maria was in fourth grade and was learning life skills from my book *Student Life Skills*. Her parents were working with her on the skill called Predict the Outcome. Maria was learning that often in her life, she could guess the results of her actions.

It wasn't hard for her to predict that when she studied math, she'd do well on her math quiz.

She was learning how predicting the outcome was useful at home, too. When she went to bed on time, she could predict that she'd have great energy for the next day.

When her parents shared this skill and language with Maria's teacher, her teacher happily used it at school. Soon, Maria was practicing her life skills every day at school, and her expertise in them grew more quickly. With this cohesive approach, the family and the school began teaching the same skill at the same time—they were literally on the same page.

The Lesson: Your children are in school about forty hours per week, so it makes a lot of sense to have you and their teachers on the same page. The continuity and predictability increase learning and a sense of safety.

The book *Student Life Skills* is a tool box of life skill sheets that have specific key words to help anchor and remind your children of the lessons.

When your children are immersed in lessons like Big Problem/Little Problem, Predict the Outcome, and Appreciate the Small Stuff with both you and their teacher, the benefits are massive.

The Takeaway: Team up with your children's teachers to deliver the same life skill lessons using the same language.

Chapter 9

Encourage Your Children to Explore Their Full Potential

As parents, we want our children to succeed. The best way to support their success is to expose them to different activities and encourage them to pursue those that tap into their strengths.

Violet

Stuart and Jenny had a beautiful daughter, Violet, who was ten years old. They loved her dearly and praised her beauty above all else.

"This is our beautiful daughter, Violet. She's the winner of our town's beauty pageant and will be competing in the state beauty pageant next week. We are so proud of her. She has a real chance of winning."

Violet smiled and said, "I hope I win because then I get my picture on a billboard in the center of town."

Stuart said, "Violet has been having some trouble

at school and making friends, but she's doing the best she can. We know she'll eventually figure it out."

Violet went on to win the pageant, and the family adored her picture on the town's billboard. Five years later, as a freshman in high school, boys began to ask Violet out on dates. Her parents supported this attention from boys, and Violet soon had a steady boyfriend. She was popular among the popular group, and all seemed to be going well.

However, she made little effort in her academics. Nor did she try to develop interests outside of being beautiful. Her parents kept telling her she was doing the best she could and that eventually she'd figure it out. Or, with her looks, at least she'd find a husband.

As time went on, however, Violet was having increasing difficulty keeping up in school. In order to inspire Violet's exploration of other strengths she might have, I encouraged her parents to utilize SP. They agreed to do so. Below is an excerpt from a conversation they had with her.

Jenny: Violet, we are so proud of you and love you so much. We know how beautiful you are, and we want to encourage you to try new things and develop new talents. What do you think you might be interested in?

Violet: I don't know. School is really hard for me.

Stuart: There are lots of ways you can be talented besides school. What are you interested in?

Violet: Well, I love fashion and hairstyles.

Stuart: Do you know you can have a career in fashion or hairstyling?

Violet: I never really thought of that! That's actually very cool.

At first, Violet was resistant to trying new things. But eventually she agreed to explore other ways she might excel, for instance, as a dancer and also in hairstyling, which she greatly enjoyed. Eventually, she dropped out of high school because she found the academic demands too stressful. But she went on to beauty school and became quite a successful hairdresser. So, it paid off for her to explore other ways she could be successful.

The Lesson: Children should be encouraged to explore all their talents and skills in order to help them succeed in life. Parents should have higher expectations for their children than "She's doing the best she can."

The Takeaway: Parents should not let their children settle for less than their full potential. They can encourage and help children find their interests and passions.

Olivia

Meeting a child's potential may require you to figure out how to help the child overcome limitations that are getting in the way of pursuing activities. For Olivia, that limitation was shyness.

John and Linda wanted to enroll Olivia in an activity in which she'd have fun, learn something interesting, and make friends. They were open to just about anything that met those criteria.

Olivia was a bit resistant, as she was nervous about failing at an activity and also about making friends since she was shy. However, the following SP conversation helped her give something new a try.

Linda: Olivia, we love you so much. We know you're really talented in lots of ways and even in some ways we haven't yet discovered. Would you be willing to join a new activity?

Olivia: Hmm, I don't know. It's hard for me to make friends, and I get nervous about making mistakes.

John: We understand that. Lots of kids feel that way—like us when we were your age. How about we first start by making a list of activities for you to consider trying?

Olivia: I guess it'd be okay if we made a list.

Linda: Great! And after that, would you be willing to go to a few of those activities just to watch?

Olivia: Sure.

I told Olivia's parents that the first step was to list the options. The activities could be at a school club, park district, or private organization. Since one of the goals was to meet other children and make friends, we picked group activities that would require inter-action among the children. That eliminated some activities, such as private music lessons, art lessons, and individual sports like swimming.

One activity popped out that excited everyone: acting lessons. It was cool, it involved other kids, and the children would spend a majority of the time interacting in a guided manner. And Olivia, who was shy, would have a script to follow with the other kids, which would allow her to interact in safe ways and experience, through acting, other ways to express herself.

Olivia and her parents observed the three acting clubs in the area. I encouraged them to not only consider the reputation of the famous director or owner of each school, but also to observe a class with each instructor who would teach Olivia. I suggested that they observe each teacher's energy, her relationship with the children, how she responded to the children when they made mistakes, and the overall vibe. Was it a competitive or cooperative experience?

After they chose one, we felt there was a high probability it would work out for Olivia.

One month into the acting lessons, Olivia reported that she mostly liked it. But some of the lessons were boring, and at times she found it difficult to remember her lines. She said she could handle those challenges and exhibited resilience regarding them. Overall, she said she liked the lessons enough to continue, and she was getting comfortable talking with the other kids before and after class.

The Lesson: As parents, it's your job to try and orchestrate activities for your children that will help them overcome limitations and find their passions.

The Takeaway: Be thoughtful in the activities you orchestrate for your children, and then take an educated chance. Live in the world of probability, not certainty. Try a lot of things.

Chapter 10

Reduce Screen Time

In my more than forty thousand hours of clinical work, along with being a father and a coach, I have seen the arc from no screens to endless hours on them. I don't like what I see. Due to technology, children have a decrease in social skills, more anxiety, less frustration tolerance, and thousands of hours of their lives wasted.

These devices act like an addicting drug, as they boost dopamine, the reward neurotransmitter, and they reinforce your children's desire to keep getting rewarded.

Of extra concern is what happens when your children become preteens and the screen time turns into social media time. When this happens, many children experience negatives such as not being included, other kids having more fun than they're having, getting cyberbullied, being a consumer of stupid information, and rating themselves based on getting "likes." Additionally concerning is that the industry uses complex algorithms meant to hook children so they continually check their devices.

Extreme Example

Lucas, an eleven-year-old boy, would play video games for 8 hours a day on school days and almost 16 hours a day on weekends. In this extreme example, that accounts for 3,744 hours a year. In less extreme examples of, say, 2 hours per school night and 4 hours on Saturday and Sunday, that still adds up to 18 hours per week or 936 hours per year.

Lucas was getting failing grades due to screen addiction. He gave up playing outside with friends so he could sit on the couch and play video games. He was also more depressed and anxious. Perhaps Lucas could have been a musician, an athlete, or amazing at any endeavor that required hours of practice and effort. He didn't care. All he wanted was to stare at a screen. He gave up everything for video games.

Lucas's parents, Michelle and Jay, tried SP to stop his addiction. The conversation went like this:

Michelle: Lucas, we love you and are concerned about all the hours you're spending playing video games.

Lucas: I'm not concerned—I love video games.

Michelle: We know you do. Do you think you can spend time doing other activities?

Lucas: No way.

Jay: What are the benefits of doing some other activity?

Lucas: None, because video games are more fun than anything else.

Jay: Well, what is the bad part of spending so much of your life playing video games?

Lucas: There is no bad part. I love it, plus I'm going to make millions of dollars as a professional video game player when I grow up. So, I don't even need school.

As you can see, SP didn't work to stop Lucas from screen time. In fact, it rarely does, and most parents have to manually regulate their children's allowed hours.

So, I suggested a more direct intervention. I had Lucas's parents install software that would turn off the video games at their control. There are several monitoring websites and software that will allow you to turn off the devices from your central hub.

We agreed to one hour on school nights and two hours on weekends. Lucas was furious at this dramatic change and felt very frustrated and anxious. However, after one month, he began to accept this new schedule, and his mood, academics, and friendships started to improve. His parents were amazed at the change and didn't realize the problems that video games had been causing their child.

The Lesson: Your children will have better lives if they spend their time finding and pursuing their interests. Free up those hours by reducing screen time.

Instead of playing video games, your children could read books, play outside, build friendships, become skilled at a sport, become fluent in a foreign language or proficient at a musical instrument, and on and on.

Furthermore, parents should know the exact games that their children are playing and perhaps even play the games themselves to get a deeper understanding of them. Also, be aware that most children watch YouTube videos of others playing video games that are often rated mature and have a lot of profanity.

The Takeaway: Reduce screen time and give your children the gift of thousands of hours to evolve in wonderful ways.

Concluding Remarks

While Socratic Parenting is not the only parenting tool you should have, it can benefit you and your children in profound ways. Your children become more autonomous, more intrinsically motivated, and happier. As for you, you will have a deeper connection with your children as well as less parenting stress.

Allow yourself to ease into SP if it's new to you. Guide your children with questions rather than offering advice all the time. Take notice of your children's more open responses and engagement with you as you use SP.

With time, you'll notice that your children are being Socratic with themselves. In other words, they will begin to ponder things rather than just dive into situations. This will help your children better evaluate goals and make choices that result in greater control over their lives, leading to greater joy and self-worth.

Appendix

Q: How do I know if my child is having serious problems? When do I know if he or she has a "disorder"? And how do I define a serious problem?

A: Defining and diagnosing mental health issues is constantly evolving, and some professionals may spend their entire career in that endeavor. As a parent, you shouldn't be burdened with the task of diagnosing your child. Rather, I suggest that you observe and be aware of your child's life—emotionally, socially, academically, medically, and physically.

Further, it's important for you to note the frequency, intensity, and duration of your child's emotional or behavioral state. Those three variables will help you better define the issue and communicate with others as needed, including doctors, teachers, tutors, and so on.

To help us all, there are developmental milestones to be aware of. We'll review them in the upcoming pages. Remember that these are general guidelines; children do not develop at the exact same rate, nor do they perform at the same level.

Diagnostic labels can help professionals set up appropriate treatments plans and help inform the team how best to help your child. But try not to get too caught up with labels, because they rarely define your entire child. Labels have changed throughout history, and children may overly identify with their label.

As you may guess, I'm not a fan of the "gifted" label for a child who scores high in academics. Any high-level achievement is noteworthy and hopefully adds joy to your child's life. Nevertheless, those achievements don't define the entirety of your child.

Developmental Milestones and Red Flags

Content adapted from the U.S. Centers for Disease Control and Prevention, "Learn the Signs. Act Early." program (www.cdc.gov/ActEarly; accessed August 1, 2019)

Age: 6 months

Social and Emotional

- Knows familiar faces and begins to know if someone is a stranger
- Likes to play with others, especially parents
- Responds to other people's emotions and often seems happy
- Likes to look at self in a mirror

Language/Communication

- Responds to sounds by making sounds
- Strings vowels together when babbling ("ah," "eh," "oh") and likes taking turns with parent while making sounds
- Responds to own name
- Makes sounds to show joy and displeasure
- Begins to say consonant sounds (jabbering with "m," "b")

Cognitive (learning, thinking, problem-solving)

- Looks around at things nearby
- Brings things to mouth
- Shows curiosity about things and tries to get things that are out of reach
- Begins to pass things from one hand to the other

Movement/Physical Development

- Rolls over in both directions (front to back, back to front)
- Begins to sit without support
- When standing, supports weight on legs and might bounce
- Rocks back and forth, sometimes crawling backward before moving forward

Act early by talking to your child's doctor if your child:

- Doesn't try to get things that are in reach
- Shows no affection for caregivers
- Doesn't respond to sounds around him
- Has difficulty getting things to mouth
- Doesn't make vowel sounds ("ah", "eh", "oh")
- Doesn't roll over in either direction
- Doesn't laugh or make squealing sounds
- Seems very stiff, with tight muscles
- Seems very floppy, like a rag doll

Age: 1

Social and Emotional

- Is shy or nervous with strangers
- Cries when mom or dad leaves
- Has favorite things and people
- Shows fear in some situations

- Hands you a book when she wants to hear a story
- Repeats sounds or actions to get attention
- Puts out arm or leg to help with dressing
- Plays games such as "peek-a-boo" and "pat-a-cake"

Language/Communication

- Responds to simple spoken requests
- Uses simple gestures, like shaking head "no" or waving "bye-bye"
- Makes sounds with changes in tone (sounds more like speech)
- Says "mama" and "dada" and exclamations like "uh-oh!"
- Tries to say words you say

Cognitive (learning, thinking, problem-solving)

- Explores things in different ways, like shaking, banging, throwing
- Finds hidden things easily
- Looks at the right picture or thing when it's named
- Copies gestures
- Starts to use things correctly; for example, drinks from a cup, brushes hair
- Bangs two things together
- Puts things in a container, takes things out of a container

- Lets things go without help
- Pokes with index (pointer) finger
- Follows simple directions like "pick up the toy"

Movement/Physical Development
- Gets to a sitting position without help
- Pulls up to stand, walks holding on to furniture ("cruising")
- May take a few steps without holding on
- May stand alone

Act early by talking to your child's doctor if your child:
- Doesn't crawl
- Can't stand when supported
- Doesn't search for things that she sees you hide
- Doesn't say single words like "mama" or "dada"
- Doesn't learn gestures like waving or shaking head
- Doesn't point to things
- Loses skills he once had

Age: 2

Social and Emotional
- Copies others, especially adults and older children
- Gets excited when with other children
- Shows more and more independence

- Shows defiant behavior (doing what she has been told not to)
- Plays mainly beside other children, but is beginning to include other children, such as in chase games

Language/Communication
- Points to objects or pictures when they are named
- Knows names of familiar people and body parts
- Says sentences with two to four words
- Follows simple instructions
- Repeats words overheard in conversation
- Points to things in a book

Cognitive (learning, thinking, problem-solving)
- Finds things even when hidden under two or three covers
- Begins to sort shapes and colors
- Completes sentences and rhymes in familiar books
- Plays simple make-believe games
- Builds towers of four or more blocks
- Might use one hand more than the other
- Follows two-step instructions such as "Pick up your shoes and put them in the closet."
- Names items in a picture book such as a cat, bird, or dog

Movement/Physical Development

- Stands on tiptoe
- Kicks a ball
- Begins to run
- Climbs onto and down from furniture without help
- Walks up and down stairs holding on
- Throws ball overhand
- Makes or copies straight lines and circles

Act early by talking to your child's doctor if your child:

- Doesn't use two-word phrases (for example, "drink milk")
- Doesn't know what to do with common things, like a brush, phone, fork, spoon
- Doesn't copy actions and words
- Doesn't follow simple instructions
- Doesn't walk steadily
- Loses skills she once had

Age: 4

Social and Emotional

- Enjoys doing new things
- Plays "Mom" and "Dad"
- Is more and more creative with make-believe play
- Would rather play with other children than alone

- Cooperates with other children
- Often can't tell what's real and what's make-believe
- Talks about what he likes and what he is interested in

Language/Communication

- Knows some basic rules of grammar, such as correctly using "he" and "she"
- Sings a song or says a poem from memory, such as the "Itsy Bitsy Spider" or "The Wheels on the Bus"
- Tells stories
- Can say first and last name

Cognitive (learning, thinking, problem-solving)

- Names some colors and some numbers
- Understands the idea of counting
- Starts to understand time
- Remembers parts of a story
- Understands the idea of "same" and "different"
- Draws a person with two to four body parts
- Uses scissors
- Starts to copy some capital letters
- Plays board or card games
- Tells you what she thinks is going to happen next in a book

Movement/Physical Development

- Hops and stands on one foot up to two seconds
- Catches a bounced ball most of the time
- Pours, cuts with supervision, and mashes own food

Act early by talking to your child's doctor if your child:

- Can't jump in place
- Has trouble scribbling
- Shows no interest in interactive games or make-believe
- Ignores other children or doesn't respond to people outside the family
- Resists dressing, sleeping, and using the toilet
- Can't retell a favorite story
- Doesn't follow three-part commands
- Doesn't understand "same" and "different"
- Doesn't use "me" and "you" correctly
- Speaks unclearly
- Loses skills he once had

Age: 5

Social and Emotional

- Wants to please friends
- Wants to be like friends
- More likely to agree with rules

- Likes to sing, dance, and act
- Is aware of gender
- Can tell what's real and what's make-believe
- Shows more independence (for example, may visit a next-door neighbor by herself [adult supervision is still needed])
- Is sometimes demanding and sometimes very cooperative

Language/Communication
- Speaks very clearly
- Tells a simple story using full sentences
- Uses future tense; for example, "Grandma will be here."
- Says name and address

Cognitive (learning, thinking, problem-solving)
- Counts ten or more things
- Can draw a person with at least six body parts
- Can print some letters or numbers
- Copies a triangle and other geometric shapes
- Knows about things used every day, like money and food

Movement/Physical Development
- Stands on one foot for ten seconds or longer
- Hops; may be able to skip
- Can do a somersault

- Uses a fork and spoon and sometimes a table knife
- Can use the toilet on his own
- Swings and climbs

Act early by talking to your child's doctor if your child:

- Doesn't show a wide range of emotions
- Shows extreme behavior (unusually fearful, aggressive, shy, or sad)
- Is unusually withdrawn and inactive
- Is easily distracted; has trouble focusing on one activity for more than five minutes
- Doesn't respond to people, or responds only superficially
- Can't tell what's real and what's make-believe
- Doesn't play a variety of games and activities
- Can't give first and last name
- Doesn't use plurals or past tense properly
- Doesn't talk about daily activities or experiences
- Doesn't draw pictures
- Can't brush teeth, wash and dry hands, or get undressed without help
- Loses skills she once had

Ages: 6–8

Developmental Milestones

Middle childhood brings many changes in a child's life. By this time, children can dress themselves, catch a ball more easily using only their hands, and tie their shoes. Having independence from family becomes more important now. Events such as starting school bring children this age into regular contact with the larger world. Friendships become more and more important. Physical, social, and mental skills develop quickly at this time. This is a critical time for children to develop confidence in all areas of life, such as through friends, schoolwork, and sports.

Here is some information on how children develop during middle childhood:

Emotional/Social Changes

Children in this age group might:

- Show more independence from parents and family
- Start to think about the future
- Understand more about their place in the world
- Pay more attention to friendships and teamwork
- Want to be liked and accepted by friends

Thinking and Learning

Children in this age group might:

- Show rapid development of mental skills
- Learn better ways to describe experiences and talk about thoughts and feelings
- Have less focus on themselves and more concern for others

Positive Parenting Tips

Following are some things you, as a parent, can do to help your child during this time:

- Show affection for your child. Recognize her accomplishments.
- Help your child develop a sense of responsibility. For example, ask him to help with household tasks, such as setting the table.
- Talk with your child about school, friends, and things she looks forward to in the future.
- Talk with your child about respecting others. Encourage him to help people in need.
- Help your child set her own achievable goals. She'll learn to take pride in herself and rely less on approval or reward from others.
- Help your child learn patience by letting others go first or by finishing a task before going out to play. Encourage him to think about possible consequences before acting.
- Make clear rules and stick to them, such as how

long your child can watch TV or when she has to go to bed. Be clear about what behavior is okay and what is not okay.

- Do fun things together as a family, such as playing games, reading, and going to events in your community.

- Get involved with your child's school. Meet the teachers and staff, and get to understand their learning goals and how you and the school can work together to help your child do well.

- Continue reading to your child. As your child learns to read, take turns reading to each other.

- Use structure to guide and protect your child, rather than punishment to make him feel bad about himself. Follow up any discussion about what not to do with a discussion of what to do instead.

- Praise your child for good behavior. It's best to focus praise more on what your child does ("You worked hard to figure this out") than on traits she can't change ("You're smart").

- Support your child in taking on new challenges. Encourage him to solve problems, such as a disagreement with another child, on his own.

- Encourage your child to join school and community groups, such as team sports, or to take advantage of volunteer opportunities.

Child Safety First

More physical ability and more independence can put children at risk for injuries from falls and other accidents. Motor vehicle crashes are the most common cause of death from unintentional injury among children this age.

- Protect your child properly in the car.
- Teach your child to watch out for traffic and how to be safe when walking to school, riding a bike, and playing outside.
- Make sure your child understands water safety, and always supervise her when she's swimming or playing near water.
- Supervise your child when he's engaged in risky activities, such as climbing.
- Talk with your child about how to ask for help when she needs it.
- Keep potentially harmful household products, tools, equipment, and firearms out of your child's reach.

Healthy Bodies

- Parents can help make schools healthier. Work with your child's school to limit access to foods and drinks with added sugar, solid fat, and salt that can be purchased outside the school lunch program.

- Make sure your child gets one hour or more of physical activity each day.

- Limit screen time for your child to no more than 1 to 2 hours per day of quality programming, at home, school, or afterschool care.

- Practice healthy eating habits and physical activity early. Encourage active play and be a role model by eating healthy at family mealtimes and having an active lifestyle.

- Make sure your child gets the recommended amount of sleep each night: for school-age children 6–12 years, 9–12 hours per 24 hours (including naps).

Ages: 9–11

Developmental Milestones

Your child's growing independence from the family and interest in friends might be obvious by now. Healthy friendships are very important to your child's development, but peer pressure can become strong during this time. Children who feel good about themselves are more able to resist negative peer pressure and make better choices for themselves. This is an important time for children to gain a sense of responsibility along with their growing independence. Also, physical changes of puberty might be showing by now, especially for girls. Another big change children need to prepare for during this time is starting middle or junior high school.

Here is some information on how children develop during middle childhood:

Emotional/Social Changes

Children in this age group might:

- Start to form stronger, more complex friendships and peer relationships. It becomes more emotionally important to have friends, especially of the same sex

- Experience more peer pressure

- Become more aware of their body as puberty approaches. Body image and eating problems sometimes start around this age.

Thinking and Learning

Children in this age group might:

- Face more academic challenges at school

- Become more independent from the family

- Begin to see the point of view of others more clearly

- Have an increased attention span

Positive Parenting Tips

Following are some things you, as a parent, can do to help your child during this time:

- Spend time with your child. Talk with her about her friends, her accomplishments, and what challenges she will face.

- Be involved with your child's school. Go to school events and meet your child's teachers.

- Encourage your child to join school and community groups, such as a sports team, or to volunteer for a charity.

- Help your child develop his own sense of right and wrong. Talk with her about risky things friends might pressure her to do, like smoking or dangerous physical dares.

- Help your child develop a sense of responsibility by involving him in household tasks like cleaning and cooking. Talk with your child about saving and spending money wisely.

- Meet the families of your child's friends.

- Talk with your child about respecting others. Encourage her to help people in need. Talk with her about what to do when others are not kind or are disrespectful.

- Help your child set his own goals. Encourage him to think about skills and abilities he would like to have and about how to develop them.

- Make clear rules and stick to them. Talk with your child about what you expect from her (behavior) when no adults are present. If you provide reasons for rules, it will help her to know what to do in most situations.

- Use structure to guide and protect your child, instead of punishment to make him feel bad about himself.

- When using praise, help your child think about her own accomplishments. Saying "You must be proud of yourself" rather than simply "I'm proud of you" can encourage your child to make good choices when nobody is around to praise her.

- Talk with your child about the normal physical and emotional changes of puberty.

- Encourage your child to read every day. Talk with him about his homework.

- Be affectionate and honest with your child, and do things together as a family.

Positive Parenting Tips

Child Safety First

More independence and less adult supervision can put children at risk for injuries from falls and other accidents. Here are a few tips to help protect your child:

- Protect your child in the car. The National Highway Traffic Safety Administration recommends that you keep your child in a booster seat until she is big enough to fit in a seat belt properly. Remember: Your child should still ride in the back seat until age twelve because it's safer there. Motor vehicle crashes are the most common cause of death from unintentional injury among children of this age.

- Know where your child is and whether a responsible adult is present. Make plans with your child for when he will call you, where you can find him, and what time you expect him home.

- Make sure your child wears a helmet when riding a bike or a skateboard or using inline skates; riding on a motorcycle, snowmobile, or all-terrain vehicle; or playing contact sports.

- Many children get home from school before their parents get home from work. It is important to have clear rules and plans for your child when she is home alone.

Healthy Bodies

- Provide plenty of fruits and vegetables; limit foods high in solid fats, added sugars, and salt; and prepare healthier foods for family meals.

- Keep television sets out of your child's bedroom. Limit screen time, including computers and video games, to no more than 1 to 2 hours a day.

- Encourage your child to participate in an hour a day of physical activities that are age-appropriate and enjoyable and that offer variety. Make sure your child is doing three types of activity: aerobic activity like running, muscle strengthening like climbing, and bone strengthening—like jumping rope—at least three days per week.

- Make sure your child gets the recommended amount of sleep each night: for school-age children 6–12 years, 9–12 hours per 24 hours (including naps)

Ages: 12–14

Developmental Milestones

This is a time of many physical, mental, emotional, and social changes. Hormones change as puberty begins. Most boys grow facial and pubic hair, and their voice deepens. Most girls grow pubic hair and breasts, and start their period. They might be worried about these changes and how they are looked at by others. This also will be a time when your teen might face peer pressure to use alcohol, tobacco products, and drugs, and to have sex. Other possible challenges include eating disorders, depression, and family problems. At this age, teens make more of their own choices about friends, sports, studying, and school. They become more independent, with their own personality and interests, although parents are still very important.

Here is some information on how young teens develop:

Emotional/Social Changes

Children in this age group might:

- Show more concern about body image, looks, and clothes
- Focus on themselves, going back and forth between high expectations and lack of confidence
- Experience more moodiness
- Show more interest in and influence by peer group
- Express less affection toward parents; sometimes might seem rude or short-tempered
- Feel stress from more challenging schoolwork
- Develop eating problems
- Feel a lot of sadness or depression, which can lead to poor grades at school, alcohol or drug use, unsafe sex, and other problems

Thinking and Learning

Children in this age group might:

- Have more ability for complex thought
- Be better able to express feelings through talking
- Develop a stronger sense of right and wrong

Positive Parenting Tips

Following are some things you, as a parent, can do to help your child during this time:

- Be honest and direct with your teen when talking about sensitive subjects such as drugs, drinking, smoking, and sex.
- Meet and get to know your teen's friends.
- Show an interest in your teen's school life.
- Help your teen make healthy choices while encouraging him to make his own decisions.
- Respect your teen's opinions and take into account her thoughts and feelings. It is important that she know you are listening to her.
- When there is a conflict, be clear about goals and expectations (like getting good grades, keeping things clean, and showing respect), but allow your teen input on how to reach those goals (like when and how to study or clean).

Child Safety First

You play an important role in keeping your child safe, no matter how old he or she is. Here are a few tips to help protect your child:

- Make sure your teen knows about the importance of wearing seat belts. Motor vehicle crashes are the leading cause of death among 12- to 14-year-olds.

- Encourage your teen to wear a helmet when riding a bike or a skateboard or using inline skates; riding on a motorcycle, snowmobile, or all-terrain vehicle; or playing contact sports. Injuries from sports and other activities are common.

- Talk with your teen about the dangers of drugs, drinking, smoking, and risky sexual activity. Ask him what he knows and thinks about these issues, and share your thoughts and feelings with him. Listen to what he says and answer his questions honestly and directly.

- Talk with your teen about the importance of having friends who are interested in positive activities. Encourage her to avoid peers who pressure her to make unhealthy choices.

- Know where your teen is and whether an adult is present. Make plans with him for when he will call you, where you can find him, and what time you expect him home.

- Set clear rules for your teen when she is home alone. Talk about such issues as having friends at the house, how to handle situations that can be dangerous (emergencies, fire, drugs, sex, etc.), and completing homework or household tasks.

Healthy Bodies

- Encourage your teen to be physically active. She might join a team sport or take up an individual sport. Helping with household tasks such as mowing the lawn, walking the dog, or washing the car also will keep your teen active.

- Mealtime is very important for families. Eating together helps teens make better choices about the foods they eat, promotes healthy weight, and gives your family members time to talk with each other.

- Limit screen time for your child to no more than 1 to 2 hours per day.

- Make sure your child gets the recommended amount of sleep each night: for teenagers 13–18 years, 8–10 hours per 24 hours (including naps).

Ages: 15–17

Developmental Milestones

This is a time of changes in how teenagers think, feel, and interact with others, and how their bodies grow. Most girls will be physically mature by now, and most will have completed puberty. Boys might still be maturing physically during this time. Your teen might have concerns about her body size, shape, or weight. Eating disorders also can be common, especially among girls. During this time, your teen is developing his unique personality and opinions. Relationships with friends are still important, yet your teen will have other interests as she develops a clearer sense of who she is. This is also an important time to prepare for more independence and responsibility; many teenagers start working, and many will be leaving home soon after high school.

Here is some information on how teens develop:

Emotional/Social Changes

Children in this age group might:

- Have more interest in romantic relationships and sexuality
- Go through less conflict with parents
- Show more independence from parents
- Have a deeper capacity for caring and sharing and for developing more intimate relationships
- Spend less time with parents and more time with friends
- Feel a lot of sadness or depression, which can lead to poor grades at school, alcohol or drug use, unsafe sex, and other problems

Thinking and Learning

Children in this age group might:

- Learn more defined work habits
- Show more concern about future school and work plans

- Be better able to give reasons for their own choices, including about what is right or wrong

Positive Parenting Tips

Following are some things you, as a parent, can do to help your teen during this time:

- Talk with your teen about her concerns and pay attention to any changes in her behavior. Ask her if she has had suicidal thoughts, particularly if she seems sad or depressed. Asking about suicidal thoughts will not cause her to have these thoughts, but it will let her know that you care about how she feels. Seek professional help if necessary.

- Show interest in your teen's school and extracurricular interests and activities, and encourage him to become involved in activities such as sports, music, theater, and art.

- Encourage your teen to volunteer and become involved in civic activities in her community.

- Compliment your teen and celebrate his efforts and accomplishments.

- Show affection for your teen. Spend time together doing things you both enjoy.

- Respect your teen's opinion. Listen to her without playing down her concerns.

- Encourage your teen to develop solutions to problems and conflicts. Help your teen learn to make good decisions. Create opportunities for him to use his own judgment, and be available for advice and support.

- If your teen engages in interactive Internet media such as games, chat rooms, and instant messaging, encourage her to make good decisions about what she posts and the amount of time she spends on these activities.
- If your teen works, use the opportunity to talk about expectations, responsibilities, and other ways of behaving respectfully in a public setting.
- Talk with your teen and help him plan ahead for difficult or uncomfortable situations. Discuss what he can do if he is in a group and someone is using drugs or if he is under pressure to have sex or is offered a ride by someone who has been drinking.
- Respect your teen's need for privacy.
- Encourage your teen to get enough sleep and exercise, and to eat healthy, balanced meals.

Safety First

You play an important role in keeping your child safe, no matter how old he or she is. Here are a few ways to help protect your child:

- Talk with your teen about the dangers of driving and how to be safe on the road. You can steer your teen in the right direction.

"Parents Are the Key" (www.cdc.gov/
parentsarethekey/index.html) has steps that
can help. Motor vehicle crashes are the leading
cause of death from unintentional injury among
teens, yet few teens take measures to reduce
their risk of injury.

- Remind your teen to wear a helmet when
riding a bike, motorcycle, or all-terrain
vehicle. Unintentional injuries resulting from
participation in sports and other activities are
common.

- Talk with your teen about suicide and pay
attention to warning signs. Suicide is the third
leading cause of death among youth fifteen
through twenty-four years of age.

- Talk with your teen about the dangers of drugs,
drinking, smoking, and risky sexual activity.
Ask him what he knows and thinks about
these issues, and share your feelings with him.
Listen to what he says and answer his questions
honestly and directly.

- Discuss with your teen the importance of
choosing friends who do not act in dangerous
or unhealthy ways.

- Know where your teen is and whether a

responsible adult is present. Make plans with her for when she will call you, where you can find her, and what time you expect her home.

Healthy Bodies

- Encourage your teen to get enough sleep and physical activity, and to eat healthy, balanced meals. Make sure your teen gets one hour or more of physical activity each day.

- Keep television sets out of your teen's bedroom.

- Encourage your teen to have meals with the family. Eating together will help your teen make better choices about the foods he eats, promote healthy weight, and give family members time to talk with each other. In addition, a teen who eats meals with the family is more likely to get better grades and is less likely to smoke, drink, or use drugs, and also less likely to get into fights, think about suicide, or engage in sexual activity.

- Make sure your child gets the recommended amount of sleep each night: for teenagers 13–18 years, 8–10 hours per 24 hours (including naps).

About the Author

Paul Sweetow, LCSW, is a graduate of the University of Chicago and has been in clinical practice for thirty years. He specializes in the study and practice of enhancing happiness and reducing unhealthy emotions. He teaches social, emotional, and organizational skills in a structured environment that emphasizes positive thinking. Paul is the author and creator of *Student Life Skills*, a life-skills workbook and program for children used by families and schools, and *The Heroic Adventures of Miles and Maria*, a series of eight children's books about friendship and personal growth. He is also a father as well as a karate world champion and seven-time consecutive national champion.

www.StudentLifeSkills.com

Public Speaking for
The Socratic Parent

**Bring the author of
The Socratic Parent
to your school, parents,
or organization for a keynote
speaking engagement!**

Paul Sweetow's upbeat, energetic presentations
are a hit at schools as well as with parents and
organizations. Audience members leave with
useful takeaways that can be used immediately
to help their children.

Contact Paul at info@TheSocraticParent.com

For FREE lessons in the online
Student Life Skills course,
go to:

www.StudentLifeSkills.com

Made in the USA
Las Vegas, NV
21 March 2022

46048796R00080